Michelangelo © MCMLXXVIII by Fabbri Editori, Milan, Italy
English Translation Copyright © by Fabbri Editori, Milan, Italy
All Rights Reserved
First U.S. Edition published 1978 by Avenel Books
distributed by Crown Publishers Inc.
Printed in Italy by Fabbri Editori, Milan.
b c d e f g h i

Library of Congress Cataloging in Publication Data
Buonarroti, Michel Angelo, 1475-1564.
Michelangelo.
1. Buonarroti, Michel Angelo, 1475-1564. I. Rasponi, Simonetta. II. Title.
N6923.B9H4 1978 709'.2'4 78-18884
ISBN 0-517-24951-0

Michelangelo, son of Ludovico Buonarroti Simoni and Francesca di Neri, was born on March 6, 1474, in the town of Caprese in the Casentino area of Tuscany. He was urged by his father toward the humanities, which he studied under the guidance of Francesco da Urbino, but soon showed a strong preference for drawing. Becoming friends with Francesco Granacci, he changed, despite opposition from his father, to the school of Ghirlandaio. In 1488 Michelangelo worked in this famous maestro's "bottega" where, according to a contract, he was to remain for three years. However, after just one year he left and went to the free school of sculpture established by Lorenzo de'Medici in the gardens of San Marco and headed by the sculptor Bertoldo, a disciple of Donatello. Noticed by Lorenzo the Magnificent (as he was known), Michelangelo was brought into his palace, where he came in contact with the great humanistic thinkers of his day—Marsilio Ficino, Pico della Mirandola, and Poliziano—and had the opportunity for cultural enrichment. There he executed his first sculptures, The Battle of the Centaurs and the Madonna della Scala.

In 1494, the year when Charles VIII of France took over Florence, Michelangelo fled to Bologna in the wake of rumors that the Medici were about to fall. After a short trip to Venice, he remained in Bologna a year as the guest of Gianfrancesco Aldovrandi, dedicating himself to literary studies and the completion of the tomb begun by the sculptor Niccolò dell'Arca.

He returned to Florence in 1501, where he began a period of intense activity. First in the field of sculpture he worked on the David, placed in 1504 in the Piazza della Signoria as a symbol of freedom, and on plans for the Duomo Apostles. In painting he worked on a large cartoon representation of the Battle of Cascina, commissioned by Gonfaloniere Pier Soderini, who had also commissioned Leonardo to do the Battle of Anghiari and the Doni Tondo. In March 1504 Pope Julius II called the artist to Rome to work on his funerary monument, which signaled major clashes between the Pope and Michelangelo. The dissension ended in 1545 with the realization of a far less important project than was called for in the original plan. This was a painful disappointment for Michelangelo, who referred to the incident as the "tragedy of the tomb."

At the same time, Michelangelo's growing obligations forced him to move constantly between Florence, Rome, Carrara, and Pietra Santa, where he personally saw to the quarrying of the marble for his sculptures. In May 1508, after a violent clash with Julius II, he signed the contract to decorate the ceiling of the Sistine Chapel, on which he worked without interruption and with great passion from the summer of that year until 1512. While occupied with the tomb of Julius II, for which he made the Slaves (now in the Louvre and in the Academy) and the Moses, Michelangelo also worked on projects for the façade of San Lorenzo, the tombs of the Medici, and the Christ for the Church of Santa Maria sopra Minerva.

In the fall of 1524 the new Medici Pope, Clement VII, had the artist begin work on the Laurentian Library and continue work on the tombs, which, begun in 1521, were finally completed in 1534, the year Michelangelo permanently settled in Rome. Toward September of that year, negotiations began for The Last Judgment, a fresco that was to cover the wall behind the altar in the Sistine Chapel. This work, which aroused so much excitement and received so much praise, was completed in 1541.

Events in Michelangelo's personal life at that time influenced his art—especially his friendship with the young Tommaso de Cavalieri, to whom Michelangelo dedicated poems and drawings, and his love for the poetess Vittoria Colonna, Marquesa of Pescara, who drew him closer to the problems of the Reform and to the ideas circulating in the milieu of Valdes.

Between 1542 and 1550 the artist worked on the frescoes for the Pauline Chapel in the Vatican. He also completed a number of sculptures, including the Florence Pietà, on which he worked in 1555, and the unfinished Rondanini Pietà.

Michelangelo was acclaimed by his contemporaries, who acknowledged him as the greatest artist of all time. He greatly influenced the art of his century; was admired without reserve by some and hated by others. Honored by popes, emperors, princes, and poets, Michelangelo died in February 1564.

Vasari recalls that "he died with great wisdom and awareness, leaving as a final testament his soul in the hands of God, his body to the earth and his belongings to his relatives."

3

"The best paintings are those which come closer to sculptured relief"

Study for the Last Judgement—Florence, Casa Buonarroti.

Michelangelo is considered one of the outstanding artists of the sixteenth century. He reached the highest degree of excellence in the three major areas of art: painting, sculpture and architecture. Through his art he interpreted the salient moments of the aesthetic evolution which brought him from the stylistic principles of the quattrocento, through the classical, to the beginnings of mannerism. Michelangelo approached perfection not through the rules of composition and space defined by his age but by reliving every formal experience in a personal way. This painful search for his own ideal was present throughout his life.

In his early studies of figures done by Giotto and Masaccio, one can already see Michelangelo's original interpretation of Ghirlandaio's teachings. His drawings stress the plasticity of the figures because, as he himself explained, "the best paintings are those which come closer to sculptured relief."

Although no other works remain from 1488, the artist's period of apprenticeship in the bottega of Domenico and David Ghirlandaio, it is clear from these studies how quickly Michelangelo attained mastery over his material and how original his stylistic conceptions were. As early as 1491, after spending just one year in Bertoldo's sculpture school in the gardens of San Marco, he sculpted *The Battle of the Centaurs Against the Lapithes,* which is now kept in the Casa Buonarroti in Florence. In 1490 he was noticed by Lorenzo the Magnificent and introduced into the Medici court, where he was introduced to the major artists and writers of the time (Poliziano, Marsilio Ficino, Pico della Mirandola). The cultural background formed at this time is already evident in *The Battle of the Centaurs.* Subject was of secondary importance to Michelangelo, who centered his attention on the dynamic effect produced by the intertwining and twisting of bodies. This interest remained a central concern in all his later work.

5

The *Madonna della Scala,* also found in the Casa Buonarroti, belongs to the same period and shows how Michelangelo tried to go beyond traditional themes. Here Michelangelo neglects Christian iconography and gives preference to the study of form and composition. This is particularly exemplified by the unusual position of the infant Christ's body.

Michelangelo never recaptured the tranquillity of the Florentine period, which ended with the death of Lorenzo the Magnificent in 1492 and the dramatic fall of the Medici. With the loss of his illustrious patron, Michelangelo moved away from the court and returned to his father's house. While there, he recalled his studies of the humanities, which taught him that classical perfection was represented in the statues of antiquity while the human body bore the mark of the Divine. He therefore decided to devote himself to the study of anatomy in the Augustinian hospital of the Church of Santo Spirito, whose prior allowed him to dissect the corpses. It was for this enlightened priest that he sculpted the wooden crucifix, today found in the Church of Santo Spirito.

With the fall of the Medici in 1494 Michelangelo left Florence. He stayed briefly in Venice, where nothing is known of his visit, and then went on to Bologna, where he was commissioned to do some statues for the completion of dell'Arca's San Domenico tomb. He sculpted the angel carrying a candelabra, which is on the right of the base of the funerary monument.

Michelangelo's stay in Bologna was a turning point in his life. He undoubtedly learned a great deal from observing the work of Jacopo della Quercia. From the low reliefs around the main doors of San Petronio, Michelangelo learned a lesson more spiritual than aesthetic. The problems of eternity obsessed him throughout his life, finding their greatest expression in the frescoes on the ceiling of the Sistine Chapel.

Breaking completely with the medieval tradition, Michelangelo embodied a new spirit which he saw represented in Jacopo della Quercia's Biblical episodes and which had already struck him in Masaccio's frescoes in the Brancacci Chapel. Man, for Michelangelo, is free in his choice of good or evil. That he chooses evil marks all of Michelangelo's life work with a sense of inevitable tragedy.

Michelangelo remained in Bologna for less than a year. He then passed a short period in the Florentine Republic before being commissioned to do a number of projects in Rome. It is in the framework of late fifteenth century Rome that Michelangelo found the ideal setting for his classically inspired sculptures. *The Bacchus,* from 1496, today found in the National Museum of Florence, is an example. In this work Michelangelo not only utilizes his perfect knowledge of anatomy, but also consciously gives the god an unsteady pose as an expression of his drunken state. There is perfect harmony in the piece; the little satyr, which appears to support the sculpture, is used as a balancing force. But the limitation of this type of purely formal research, even if sophisticated, did not satisfy Michelangelo. And the passionate religiousness of his work was soon to appear.

In 1498 the artist was officially commissioned to execute the funerary monument of the French cardinal, Jean de Lagraulas. This first of his many representations of the *Pietà* was completed in 1499 and today is found in Saint Peter's Basilica. In this work the classical theme is abandoned and even the highly polished marble, with its extraordinary clarity, is used by Michelangelo to arrive at a purity and spiritual beauty that soften the tragedy and agony of the theme. The Madonna's face—so gentle and sad—is made to appear extremely young, her youth symbolizing the virginity of her soul. This aroused criticism among Michelangelo's contemporaries since he had evidently broken with the traditional iconography. However, few works of art evoke such intense religious and spiritual emotions.

On his return to Florence in 1501, Michelangelo, already a well-known artist, received numerous important commissions of which

Studies from Giotto's figures—Paris, The Louvre.

he completed only a part. For his unfinished works, scholars have offered explanations ranging from Michelangelo's own touchy temperament to his clashes with patrons who did not understand him. Many of the patrons were interested only in the functional purpose of the works they commissioned, and it was emotionally exhausting for Michelangelo to be subjected to this while trying to create an artistic masterpiece. But the main reason he was unable to complete everything requested of him was his way of working, which made it impossible for him to delegate work, as was the tradition in the quattrocento—Raphael being a notable example. Michelangelo would never have been able to prepare a model that his assistants could refer to, since his works consisted of changes of positions and gradual elaborations. He was continually retouching, changing positions, gradually and intuitively elaborating as the material revealed the form he was searching for.

Michelangelo's very polished *Bruges Madonna* shows the important tie between formal research and the artistic ideal. But it is even more evident in the *David,* which was commissioned in 1501 by the Florentine government. The statue was first placed in front of the Palazzo della Signoria, where a copy now stands. The original is in the Academy. In this work, Michelangelo attains a synthesis which is the most powerful and characteristic of all his works. The statue is a powerful form inspired by the classical tradition. He represents the biblical figure filled with moral significance and internalizes the strength and physical beauty that became the image of vitality and spiritual courage. It is the expression of Michelangelo's heroic conception of man's confrontation with life.

The same controlled energy is found in Michelangelo's first pictorial work, the *Doni Tondo,* which dates back to 1504. In this painting the artist concentrates his energetic and clear plastic language on the study of composition and form. He uses color to emphasize the form and disposition of the figures; and, breaking away from the usual Christian iconography, he creates an impression of strength and energy through the intertwining and unwinding of bodies into lines and spirals.

Two other works of art belong to the same period—the sculptures *Pitti Tondo* and *Taddei Tondo.* However, they are less significant than the *Doni Tondo* to Michelangelo's overall artistic evolution.

The Battle of Cascina is infinitely more important in this respect because of the uproar it created and the influence it had on Michelangelo's contemporaries. In 1504 the gonfalonier of the Florentine Republic, Pier Soderini, entrusted Michelangelo to paint a war scene in the Sala del Gran Consiglio on the opposite wall from where Leonardo was supposed to represent the *Battle of Anghiari.* Michelangelo's theme came from an episode of the war of 1364 between the Florentines and the inhabitants of Pisa. The Florentine soldiers, surprised by the enemy as they were bathing in the Arno River near Cascina, were saved by Manno Donati's cry of alarm. They feld from the river bank and prepared for the battle, which they eventually won. The subject matter lent itself perfectly to Michelangelo's expressive talents. The extreme variety of movements, the intertwining of bodies, the architectural complexity marked, even more than the *Doni Tondo,* the beginnings of a new manneristic sensitivity. Only a cartoon form of the work was ever executed and exhibited, along with some of Michelangelo's preparatory drawings. They raised many outcries because of their novelty but were also widely copied and studied by his contemporaries.

Summoned by Pope Julius II, Michelangelo left for Rome in 1505, enticed by the invitation to construct the pope's mausoleum. This aroused the artist's enthusiasm, but the pope continually changed his mind. Disillusioned and exasperated, Michelangelo impulsively returned to Florence. It was in 1506, following the mediation of important and powerful people, that Michelangelo agreed to make peace with Julius II. Upon his return to

8 Rome, still not having abandoned his idea of a mausoleum, the ar-

tist was forced by the authoritative pope to paint the ceiling of the Sistine Chapel.

Michelangelo did not begin this work until May of 1508, when the contract was finally signed. On October 31, 1512, to everyone's amazement, the first mass was celebrated under the new ceiling. Four years of superhuman effort and increasing fatigue and tension, Michelangelo had achieved the supreme expression of his artistic language. Controlling his own existential torment, he expressed his own conception of man's destiny and the mystery of the universe through the pictorial representation of the tragedy of the first sin and the ruthlessness of the punishment. His cheerful tones and faith in his own ability, as well as in the world of visible forms are never again seen in his works, where the painful internal struggle between inspiration and expression is always more visible.

The painting on the ceiling of the Sistine Chapel is grandiose and completely new in concept. The figures, separated from the structural setting but stressed and underlined in an architectural framework, play the dominant role. The work has been defined as "animated architecture." The theme represented by Michelangelo, the story of the world before the coming of Christ, is divided into three areas. The central part is made up of nine panels illustrating the origin of the world, of humanity, and of sin and its consequences. The next area, which encloses the central part, depicts the prophets and sibyls who come to announce the coming of Christ. The third area, made up of triangles, lunettes, and panache, represents stories of Christ's forefathers and the salvation of Israel. The nude figures adorning the central area allegorically mediate between God and man, unifying the two parts.

The overwhelming effect of the work does not hide the powerful, plastic form and gestures of the individual figures; they are the real stars of this masterpiece.

Finally, after recovering from his years of exhausting work on the Sistine Chapel, Michelangelo was ready to begin work on Julius II's tomb. He was once again frustrated in the realization of his dream, first by the death of the pope and then by many new and pressing commissions. The only part of his original, ambitious plan that was executed was the monumental statue of *Moses*, completed in 1516 and housed today in the Church of San Pietro in Vincoli. The *Moses* is similar in concept to the Sistine figures both in its imposing size and in the energy that emanates from the sculpture's contained expression and sullen stare.

In 1520 Michelangelo began work on his first architectural commission: the Sacrestia Nuova of San Lorenzo in Florence, built to hold the remains of the Medici family and therefore commonly referred to as the Medici Chapel. The project was modified a few times and took Michelangelo fourteen years to complete, including interruptions. The chapel is a square enclosed by a cupola; the walls are embellished with various architectural elements such as ornamental columns and fake windows. In the center are two funerary monuments, one of Giuliano and one of Lorenzo de Medici, depicted as heros of antiquity. In the chapel, where man was usually invited to meditate on his own mortality and the inexorable passage of time, Michelangelo represents an entirely new concept: the universal meaning of immortality, combining the pagan glorification of man with the Christian belief in eternity.

The innovative role Michelangelo played in the field of architecture comes out even more clearly in his second architectural work, the Laurentian Library, begun in 1524 and completed by Vasari in 1552. This work, rich with architectural motifs that serve no specific purpose, refutes the idea of a pre-established balance and harmony, thereby showing the first signs of manneristic architecture.

In addition to some constructions and their related drawings belonging to this Florentine period there are also the four unfinished statues, the *Prisoners*, now in the Academy in Florence. They are perfect examples of Michelangelo's belief that forms are already present in the material and that it is the artist's duty to discern them and free them.

9

Madonna with St. Anne and Child—
Oxford, Ashmolean Museum.

contrasts the balanced structure of the ceiling itself, was altogether contrary to traditional rules of proportion and perspective. The figures are grouped together or dispersed without any apparent regard for rules of composition. It is this violent movement which Michelangelo uses to represent the drama of God's punishment. In this work the artist attained the ultimate limits of the Renaissance; he no longer is attracted by nature or beauty, which were the unifying force in his earlier works. From this point on, Michelangelo's artistic language became more and more spiritual.

His last works, the frescoes in the Pauline Chapel, especially the *Conversion of Saint Paul* and the *Crucifixion of Saint Peter,* shows Michelangelo's continuing break with tradition.

In 1537 he was appointed architect of the Apostolic palaces, and during the same time he completed the façade and court of the Palazzo Farnese. A little later, in 1546 and 1547, he worked on the urban plan for the Piazza del Campidoglio.

Saint Peter's Basilica is his last and greatest architectural work. Michelangelo used Bramante's original plan for the Basilica but elaborated upon it, giving it his own personal touch. The original plan in the form of a Greek cross was reduced in size so as to focus more attention on the central part of the building. This area is enclosed by a cupola giving it the feeling of indefinite space, while the monumental external structure makes it the largest Christian temple.

Michelangelo devoted his last years entirely to sculpture, his preferred art. In 1555 he smashed the *Pietà* (now restored and in the Cathedral of Florence) in a fit of anger because he realized the impossibility of achieving the ideal he sought.

The Palestrina Pietà, today in the Academy in Florence, was left unfinished. In the last days of his life, Michelangelo went on striving for perfection; in the Rondanini Pietà he left us the image of his own inner conflict.

In 1534 Michelangelo returned to Rome to paint the entire wall behind the altar in the Sistine Chapel. From that time on he remained in the capital. When the fresco, *The Last Judgment,* was completed in 1541 it was received with both deep admiration and harsh criticism. The novelty and boldness of the painting, which

Index of the illustrations

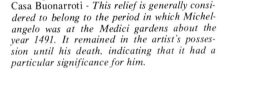

XII - Study for the battle of the nudes - Oxford, Ashmolean Museum - *It seems to be certain, a hypothesis suggested by authoritative critics since the beginning of the 19th century, that this drawing was a preparatory sketch for the large fresco of the Battle of Cascina, that was planned for the Salone dei Cinquecento in the Palazzo Vecchio for which Michelangelo made only the cartoon.*

XIII - Holy Family - Florence, Uffizi - *The Doni Tondo was perhaps made for the wedding of Agnolo Doni with Maddalena Strozzi, between 1503 and 1505. This is the first known of Michelangelo's paintings, but already one can see that painting is for him "better when the element of relief is emphasized." The abstract color, in fact, follows the athletic contortions of the figures.*

XIV - Pitti Tondo - (marble) - Florence, Bargello - *The date of this tondo (made for Bartolomeo Pitti) is not certain, but most likely it was sculpted a short time after 1503 when the sculpture of David was finished, and before 1505 when the artist was called to Rome. It was probably made a short time before the Taddei Tondo.*

XV - Pitti Tondo - (detail of the Child) - (marble) - Florence, Bargello - *The face demonstrates how Michelangelo used a hooked chisel, leaving impressed on the marble the directional signs that defined the heightening and falling of the surface with a technique similar to that used in drawing.*

XVI - Study for the figure of an apostle - Florence, Uffizi, Gabinetto Disegni e Stampe - *Several critics believe that this is a preparatory drawing for one of the statues of the apostles that Michelangelo was commissioned to make for the Opera del Duomo of Florence. The influence of classical sculpture on Michelangelo is evident in this drawing.*

XVII - Study of figures and embellishments - Florence, Uffizi, Gabinetto Disegni e Stampe - *This drawing contains numerous sketches referring to several works that were projected by Michelangelo during the first years of the 16th century. One can, in fact, identify some parts of the Bruges Madonna and in the figure in the center one of the nudes for the Battle of Cascina.*

XVIII - Study for a Virile Nude - Haarlem, Teylers Museum - *This figure, which contorts toward the left, is clearly connected to the figure of a soldier armed with a club in the Battle of Cascina, which can be seen only in the etchings and copies of his cartoon made by Michelangelo's contemporaries.*

XIX - Study for a Virile Nude - Florence, Casa Buonarroti - *Numerous critics have maintained that Michelangelo's inspiration for this nude came from a late period Roman sarcophagus representing the labors of Hercules that was probably conserved at the Lateran Museum.*

XX - Partial view of the ceiling - Rome, Sistine Chapel - *The official commission to decorate the ceiling of the Sistine Chapel was given to Michelangelo on May 10, 1508, and as can be read in the artist's letters and in the biographies, he began work on the project that day.*

XXI - Cumaean Sibyl - Rome, Sistine Chapel - *The somber old age of the Sibyl, with the grave and solemn gestures of her arms and legs, is similar to the old prophets of the ceiling of the Sistine Chapel, and to the Moses of the tomb of Julius II. The matching of yellow and grey-violet colors on the monochromatic tones of the background balance the plasticity of the drawing with the rest of the work.*

XXII - Judith and Holofernes - Rome, Sistine Chapel - *The scenes of the miracles of the salvation of Israel are grouped in the four angular pendentives of the ceiling of the Chapel, with a brief narration that takes into account the culminating moments of each event. The style is solemn and concise, but it expresses the underlying subtleness of the color, as can be seen in the robes of the two women.*

XXIII - The Torment of Amon - Rome, Sistine Chapel - *This episode as well represents a scene illustrating the salvation of Israel. It reveals Michelangelo's ability to express the greatest dramatic moment of the episode. The large nude in the center is the pictorial equivalent, but with a greater dramatic action, of the sorrowful Prisons of the tomb of Julius II.*

XXIV - XXV - Scenes of the Creation - Rome, Sistine Chapel - *The scenes of the creation of the world and of mankind, the last that were executed on the ceiling of the Chapel, express a greater intensity of color and a more complex spatial structure when confronted with the previous scenes of the Drunkenness of Noah and the Deluge. The work on the ceiling was done from 1508 to 1512.*

XXVI - The Prophet Jonah - Rome, Vatican City, Sistine Chapel - *The figure of this prophet, perfectly placed within the rigid criteria of symmetrical conformity that characterizes the fresco of the ceiling, is placed in opposition to the prophet Zachariah: the two are at the extremes of the central panels.*

XXVII - Abijah: an Ancestor of Christ - Rome, Sistine Chapel - *This, with other figures, comprises the series of Christ's Ancestors that Michelangelo painted in the frescoes, dividing them into families of three people, as that of Christ's, within the triangles and in the lunettes that surround the central strips of the ceiling.*

XXVIII-XXIX - Drunkenness of Noah - Rome, Sistine Chapel - *This is the last scene in the logical succession of the narration that Michelangelo painted in the central panels of the ceiling, and that illustrates the theme of the history of the world before the coming of Christ, but that Michelangelo executed prior to the others.*

13

XXX - Libyan Sibyl - Rome, Sistine Chapel - *The Sibyls and the Prophets that announce the coming of the Saviour incarnate, in their varied articulated positions, the phases of hope and waiting for the whole of humanity. Next to them, placed within the lunettes, are the figures of the Ancestors of Christ who testify, in somber and low-keyed tones, to the squalor of an existence deprived of Divine Revelation.*

XXXI - The Persian Sibyl - Rome, Sistine Chapel - *The old Sibyl, with her athletic body of an ancient statue, stands out within the context of the Chapel's ceiling due to the bold use of the counterlight around the head. The hooked profile in the shadow, emphasized by the light tones of the robes, anticipates some of the extraordinary effects of* The Last Judgment *with its mannerist overtones.*

XXXII - The Universal Deluge - Rome, Sistine Chapel - *The deluge, which in the Biblical story follows the episodes of the creation of the world, was the first subject that Michelangelo executed, immediately following the first studies for the division of the entire work. As a result, even though the theme is dramatically complex, the style is very similar to the Doni Tondo.*

XXXIII - Dying Slave - (marble) - Paris, Musée du Louvre - *This figure and its complement (plate X) were sculpted for the Tomb of Julius II. Too big for the reduced size of the finished mausoleum (1554), they were donated by Michelangelo to Roberto Strozzi, who in turn offered them to Francis I, king of France.*

XXXIV - Moses - (marble) - Rome, S. Pietro in Vincoli - *The figure, conceived to remain isolated on the upper part of the tomb, is now found in the central niche - that in the final plan was placed against a wall - and is surrounded by Rachel and Leah, the only two other sculptures of the tomb made by Michelangelo.*

XXXV - Moses - detail of the head - (marble) - Rome, S. Pietro in Vincoli - *Sculpted in 1513, the sculpture of Moses is perhaps the best known figure created by Michelangelo. This is justified by the intense psychological force of its proud look, by the twisted position of the head, and by the powerful hands - one of which grasps the beard.*

XXXVI - Tomb of Giuliano de' Medici - (marble) - Florence, S. Lorenzo, Medici Chapel - *Beneath the statue of Giuliano seated, are the allegorical figures representing Night and Day. Supine figures of the river gods were planned to be placed beneath the sarcophagus, but none were ever sculpted.*

XXXVII - Giuliano de' Medici - detail of the head (marble) - Florence, S. Lorenzo, Medici Chapel - *Giuliano de' Medici, duke of Nemours, the son of Lorenzo il Magnifico, died in 1516. It seems that the idea of erecting a chapel in his honor, as well as for the other members of the family, came from Cardinal Giulio de' Medici toward the year 1520.*

XXXVIII - Medici Virgin - (marble) - Florence, S. Lorenzo, Medici Chapel - *The Madonna adapts itself very well to the style of the Allegories in the Medici Chapel, and it was probably meant to be placed in its actual position at the far end of the wall in the Tomb of Lorenzo, which was never finished.*

XXXIX - Dawn - (marble) - Florence, S. Lorenzo, Medici Chapel - *The allegories of the Medici Chapel are the only female nudes that Michelangelo ever sculpted: those of Dawn and Night. Dawn is much more beautiful than many of the female nudes sculpted in antiquity: her body is slim and her face has an extraordinary elegance.*

XL - Victory - (marble) - Florence, Palazzo Vecchio - *This group was sculpted for one of the niches of the mausoleum of Pope Julius II. The ideal, based on this type of composition, of a spiral figure tapered like a pyramid with its base at the apex, was to become a fundamental precept of the sculptural theory of the 15th century.*

XLI - Young Slave - (marble) - Florence, Academy - *The composition of this Slave seems to have been based on that of the Dying Slave. It is most likely that the figure was planned as a substitute for the original statue, which was too small for the new arrangement of the Tomb of Julius II, of 1516.*

XLII - Study of nudes and Madonna with Child - London, British Museum - *The group of nudes, that perhaps can be traced to a study for the Battle of Cascina, is clearly of classical inspiration. The figure in the center can be connected to the Apollo Belvedere, while in the figure on the right one can recognize a study of the Castor and Pollux. The sketch on the left traces out the Bruges Madonna.*

XLIII - Study of a head in foreshortening - Florence, Casa Buonarroti - *Usually, Michelangelo concentrated his attention on the studies of bodies, and it is for this very reason that this drawing stands out. Due to the way that the figure is drawn, and the research in the foreshortening, critics have associated the drawing to either the Doni Tondo or Jonah in the Sistine Chapel.*

XLIV - Architectural studies and studies for fortifications - Florence, Uffizi, Gabinetto Disegni e Stampe, from Casa Buonarroti - *These two drawings can certainly be attributed to the last Florentine period, which began in 1520 and ended in 1534 with Michelangelo's settling in Rome. We can observe in the first drawing a study for the façade of S. Lorenzo, while in the second is the plan for the fortification of the gate of the Prato d'Ognissanti.*

XLV - Reading room - Florence, Laurentian Library - *Michelangelo began working on the Laurentian Library in 1524, but due to other commissions, or to the political upheavals of the years that followed, he never finished the work. It was continued by Vasari and Ammannati, who followed and respected the original plan.*

XLVI-XLVII - The Last Judgment - Rome, Sistine Chapel - *The last wall of the Sistine Chapel was executed between 1536 and 1541, but the first project for it goes back to the end of 1534. Michelangelo conceives the scene as a very large tapestry in which the tragic forms contort and join in a "manner that is between the difficult and the beautiful, very beautiful and very difficult" (Vasari).*

XLVIII - The Last Judgment - (detail of a group of the damned) - Rome, Sistine Chapel - *The damned are the most dramatic figures of The Last Judgment. The tragic expressions of the damned are almost grotesque; he gives free rein to the forms of the demons that, reduced to decorative elements, would supply an extensive repertoire to the eccentricities of a certain type of mannerist painting.*

XLIX - The Last Judgment - (detail of Christ the Judge) - Rome, Sistine Chapel - *The ideal perfection of Christ and the tragic irremediability of his gesture had partially blocked Michelangelo's hand, and what results is a rhetorical and euphemistic figure. The Virgin, gathered at his side in her function of intermediary, does not relieve the preconception of the group.*

L-LI - The Angels Awake the Dead - (detail of the Last Judgment) - Rome, Sistine Chapel - *The influence of the Holy Scriptures is evident in this wall fresco, as it is in the frescoes on the ceiling, but the 24 years that passed from the time that Michelangelo began to paint the ceiling, and the influence of the Lutheran Reformation, clearly show the artist's spiritual and religious evolution.*

LII - The Last Judgment - (detail of the resurrection of the flesh) - Rome, Sistine Chapel - *In the lower part of the Judgment, contrasting with the boat of the damned, is found the scene of the resurrection of the flesh, based on medieval conceptions. The representation of the "afflicted" in the grotesque figures of the damned, emphasized through the effects of the light, becomes almost hallucinatory.*

LIII - Charon's Boat - (detail of the Last Judgment) - Rome, Sistine Chapel - *The figure of Charon, who transports the damned to Hell on his boat, was continually criticized by Michelangelo's contemporaries, who thought that it was an act of heresy to insert a pagan figure within a Christian work.*

LIV - Conversion of St. Paul - Rome, Pauline Chapel - *The execution of the fresco, of which a detail is here reproduced, was made between 1542 and 1545. Michelangelo intensified to an extreme the representation of the "afflicted," but he also emphasized the chromatic gradations and the softness of the materials, already hinted at in other parts of the Sistine Chapel.*

LV - Crucifixion of St. Peter - Rome, Pauline Chapel - *This is the last painting of Michelangelo, executed between 1546 and 1550. The conception of the perspective, almost an aerial view, and the use of the half-figures in the foreground, prefigure certain compositional schemes of the late mannerist period. But what is especially new is the landscape with its incumbent melancholy.*

LVI - Rondanini Pietà - (marble) - Milan, Castello Sforzesco - *The theme of the Pietà was particularly close to Michelangelo, who used it four times in his work. This marble group, the last of the four, and the "least finished" in accordance with the esthetic evolution of the artist, is also the last work that Michelangelo applied himself to, having worked on it up to six days before his death.*

LVII - Pietà - (marble) - Florence, Duomo - *The Pietà was probably begun when the Lives of Vasari was first published in 1550, where it is mentioned that the work was begun. It was probably made for Michelangelo's own tomb, but it was accidentally broken before 1555. The pieces were conserved.*

LVIII - View of the Basilica and the Piazza of St. Peter's - Rome, Vatican City - *Succeeding Antonio da Sangallo, the younger, in the construction of St. Peter's as the chief architect, Michelangelo began his work in 1546, reconsidering Bramante's project that had been rejected by his predecessor.*

LIX - Façade of the Basilica of St. Peter's - Rome, Vatican City - *Michelangelo wanted to emphasize to the utmost the magnificence of this building by enriching the façade with a series of Corinthian pilasters and columns, and with an attic animated by windows, niches, and pediments that stressed the monumentality of the temple.*

LX - Drawing of the exterior and of the vertical section of the Basilica of St. Peter's - *These drawings emphasize the sought-after chiaroscuro effect caused by the wealth of architectonic elements and the originality of the design that, respecting the plan of the Greek cross, reduces the arms in order to concentrate the interior space about the majestic square ambulatory that supports the dome.*

LXI - Interior of the dome of St. Peter's - Rome, Vatican City - *In working out his architectural masterpiece, Michelangelo kept many of the elements of Bramante's project, but he transformed them, inspired by Brunelleschi's dome of Santa Maria del Fiore in Florence. He gave the dome a vigorous expansion by avoiding a hemispherical shape; it became higher and was upheld by an enormous drum animated by a double row of columns.*

LXII - Piazza del Campidoglio - Rome - *The urbanistic arrangement of the Piazza, entrusted to Michelangelo in 1546 by the Vatican, was to find a more harmonious solution between the still medieval aspects of the Piazza of the period, and the new Renaissance appearance that the city was assuming.*

LXIII - Piazza del Campidoglio seen from above - Rome - *Fitting into the new architectonic concept of the 15th century, Michelangelo gave the Piazza the illusion of spaciousness and an almost geometrical harmony by his original design for the paving of the square that perfectly responded to the scenic exigencies of the times.*

15

III

IV

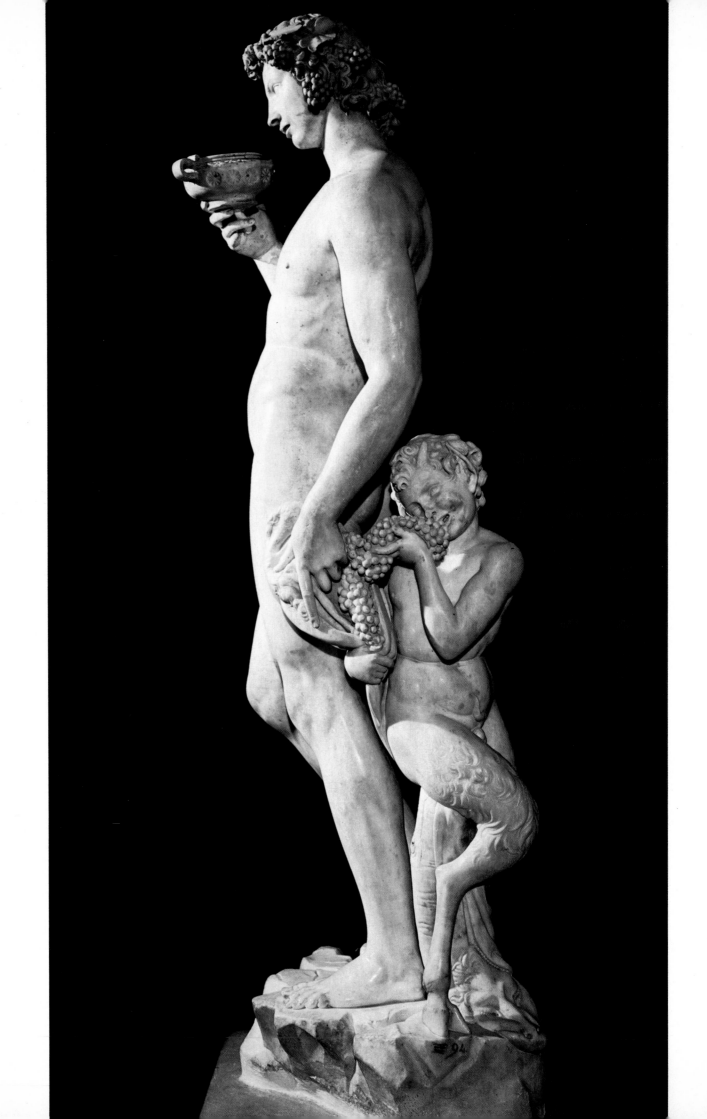

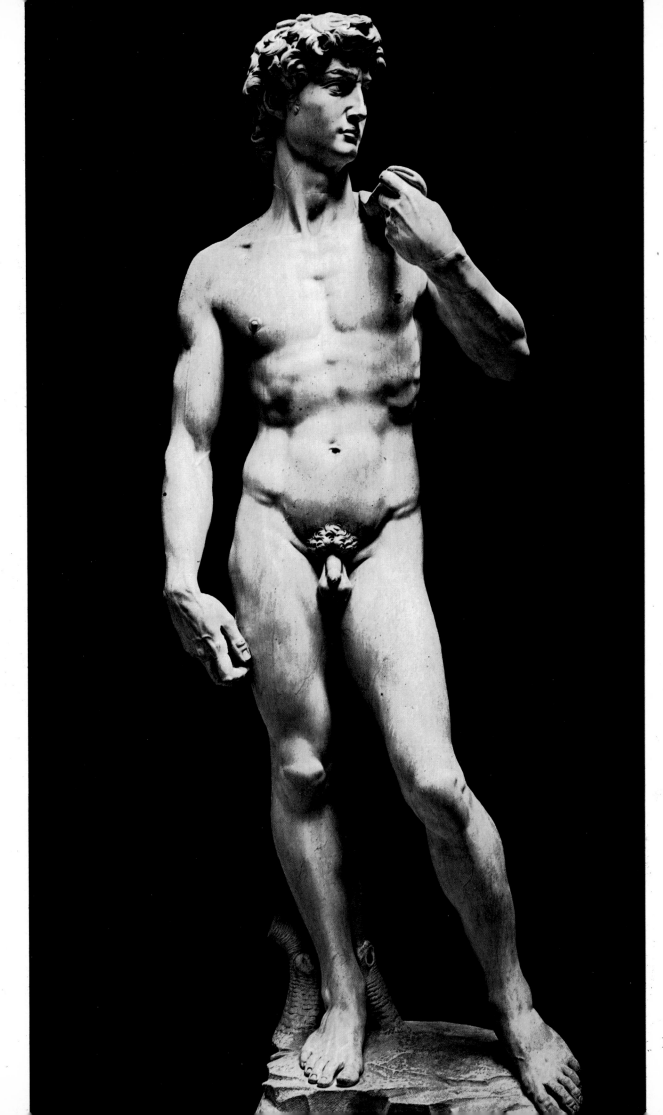

IX

X

XII

XIII

XIV

XV

XVI

XVII

XVIII

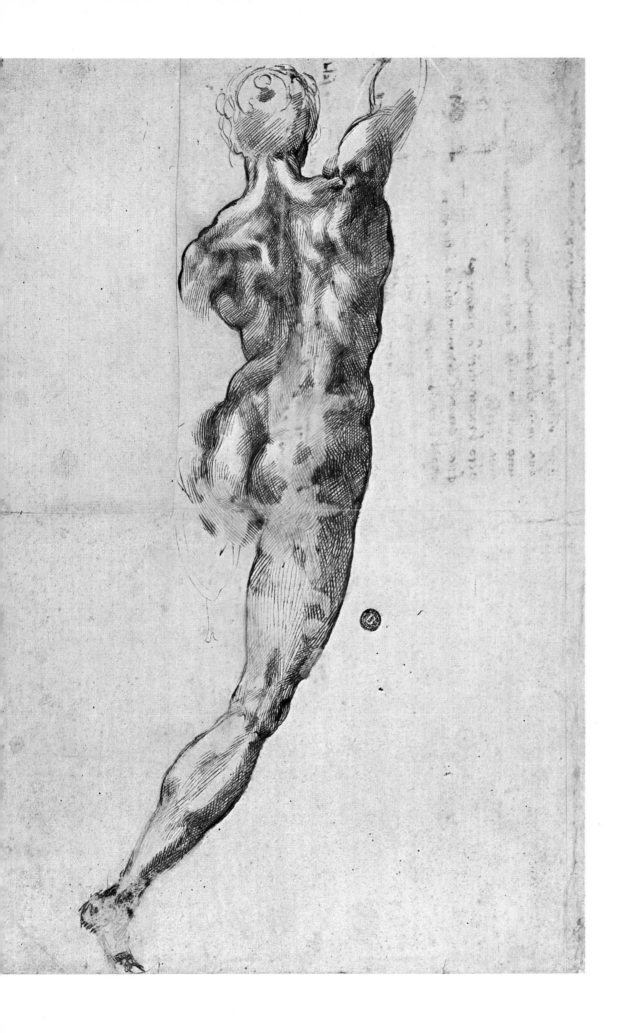

XXI

IONAS

XXVII

LIBICA

XXXI

XXXII

XXXVII

XL

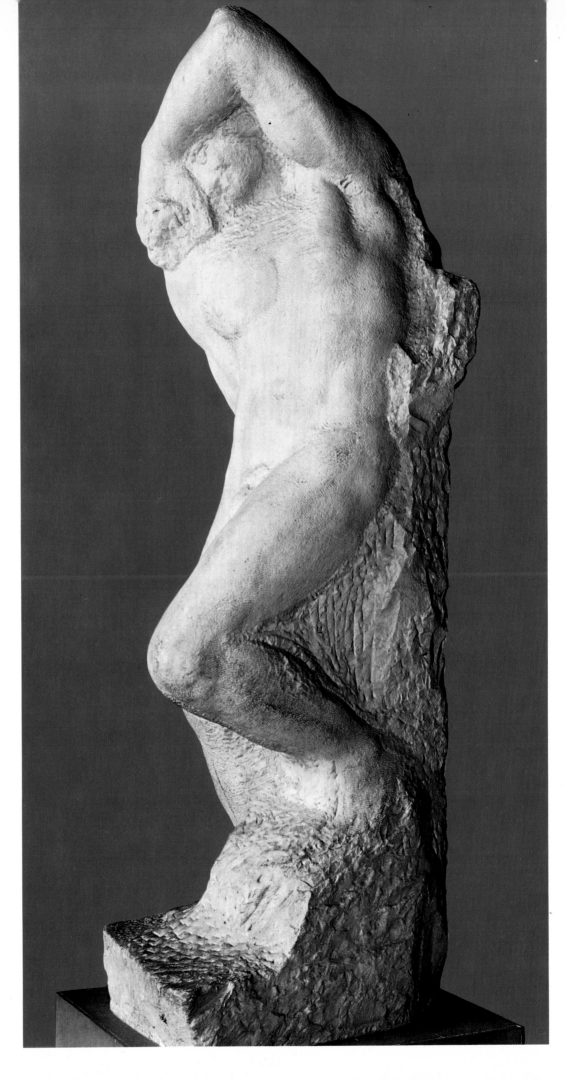

XLIII

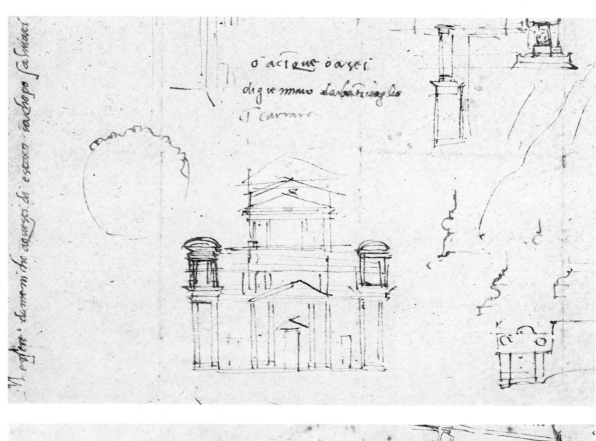

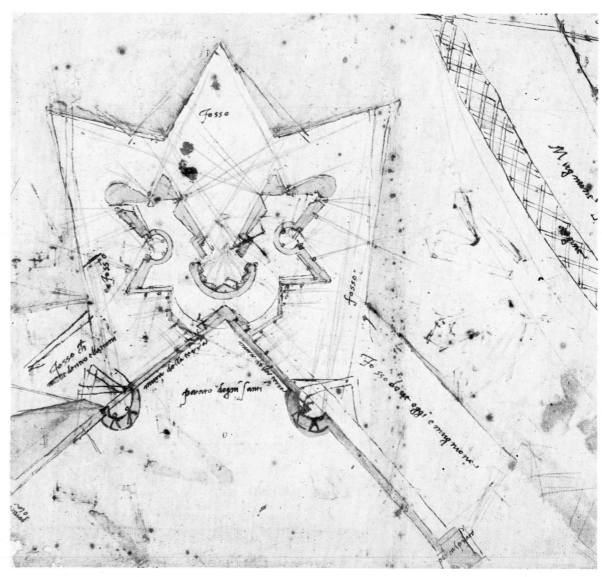

XLVIII

XLIX

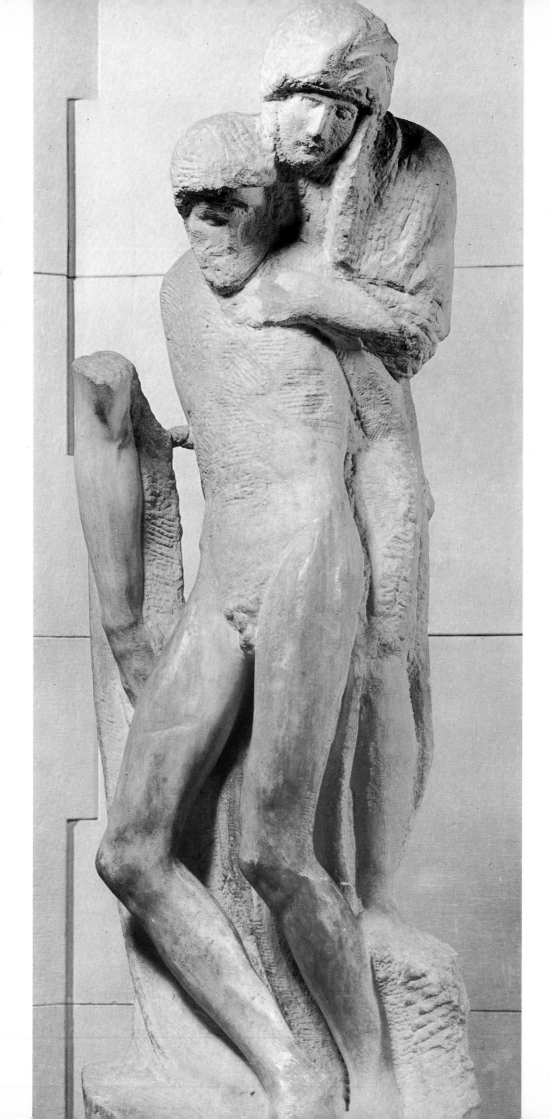

LVI

LVIII

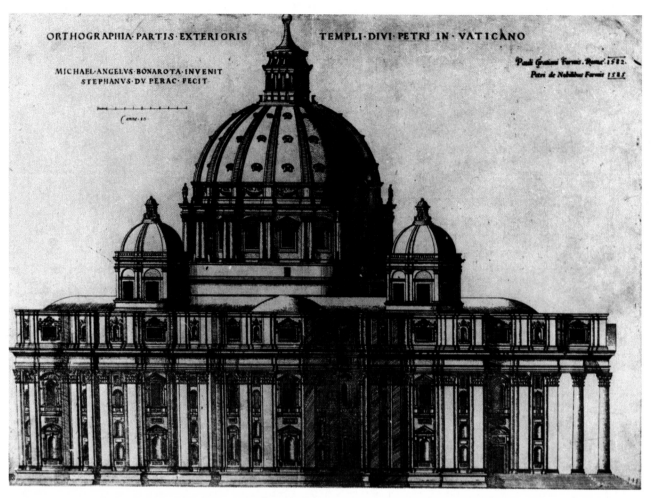

ORTHOGRAPHIA·PARTIS·EXTERIORIS   TEMPLI·DIVI·PETRI·IN·VATICANO

MICHAEL·ANGELVS·BONAROTA·INVENIT
STEPHANVS·DV·PERAC·FECIT

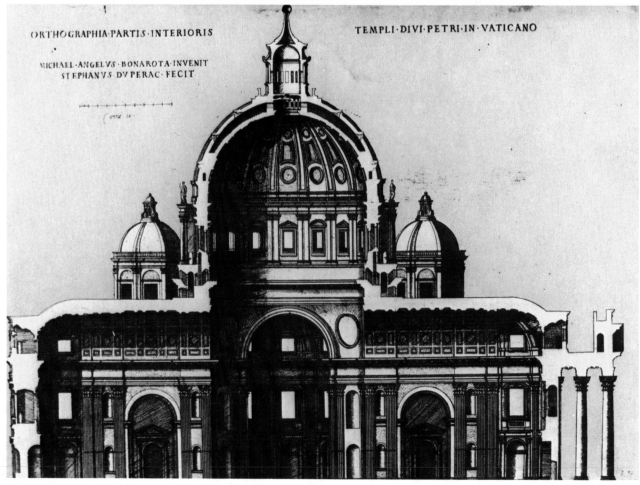

ORTHOGRAPHIA·PARTIS·INTERIORIS   TEMPLI·DIVI·PETRI·IN·VATICANO

MICHAEL·ANGELVS·BONAROTA·INVENIT
STEPHANVS·DV·PERAC·FECIT